LifeLessons:
Gratitude

By Lenore Skomal

CIDER MILL
PRESS

BOOK
PUBLISHERS

Kennebunkport, Maine

This book is dedicated to my husband, who has taught me the greatest
LifeLesson of all--how to accept love.

ISBN: 1-933662-03-4

This book may be ordered by mail from the publisher.
Please include $3.50 for postage and handling.

Please support your local bookseller first!

Books published by Cider Mill Press Book Publishers are available
at special discounts for bulk purchases in the United States
by corporations, institutions, and other organizations.
For more information, please contact the publisher.

Cider Mill Press Book Publishers
"Where good books are ready for press"
12 Port Farm Road
Kennebunkport, Maine 04046

Visit us on the web!
www.cidermillpress.com

Package Cover Design by: Tilly Grassa and Lana Mullen
Design by: Tilly Grassa
Typography: Goudy, Rotis Sans Serif

Printed in China
1 2 3 4 5 6 7 8 9 0
First Edition

CONTENTS

Chapter I

Gratitude

"If the only prayer life was thank you,

you ever said in your

hat would suffice."

— Meister Eckhart, Christian mystic

It is the place within your soul where all blessings are born. The hallowed spot, that if nurtured and visited often, will open the doors to the majesty of possibility. This place dwells within each and every one of us. But the randomness of life, its anguishes and upheavals, can obscure the path to its door. While we can go there any time we would like, many of us choose not to. We choose to stand a good distance away and wait for it to come to us. After all, it's easier to complain about life than it is to unconditionally embrace it. That place in our souls which can make our lives so much better and fuller is called gratitude.

Miracles happen every day. But so few of us see them. Maybe we are just too busy with reality. Better put, maybe we just don't want to try to see them. Understanding miracles requires a repositioning of self. It requires some work on our part. Miracles have to be met halfway, and it would be so much simpler if they were heralded with trumpets, bursts of ethereal light and grand aplomb. In Jainism, it is said that "the gods do not announce themselves." That is, the amazing is often masked by the mundane. So in order to see that which is miraculous we need to seek it. We have to be open to it. We have to twist the focus on our life lens so that we not only view all that is unfolding around us, but actively see it and appreciate it.

For too many of us, life is something that just happens to us. Irrationally, we feel not only that we have no control at all, but also that we can impose conditions. Unless life unfolds in a prescribed manner of our choosing, misinterpretation coupled with despair is how we greet life. After being battered about by life's unpredictability, something else gets beaten out of us. That something is hope.

J aded and tossed about, it is easy to reduce living to a day-to-day struggle to make do. If those days are highlighted with bright spots and happy moments, great. But more often than not, many of us tend to view life as an arduous, uphill journey, granting us no control over our destiny or the environment around us.

Being open to the realm of possibility is indeed tough when you feel victimized, as if everyone is against you. When life is bearing down on you and you feel like Atlas with the weight of the world on your shoulders, and all you want to do is shrug, how can you possibly see the beauty and magic around you?

The secret is as old as the universe, as mystics, prophets, theologians, and humanitarians have discovered. It is cultivating a life state of gratitude. Contrary to the pop phrase, gratitude is not merely an attitude. It is so much more. In its most cultivated, divine form, gratitude is a state of being. It emanates from the core of your existence and transforms the way you see the world and everything in it.

Gratitude is the cornerstone of all the world's religions, including Christianity, Judaism, Islam, Buddhism, Shintoism and Jainism... Whether it be praise and honor to a monotheistic God, to multiple spirits of nature, to each other or to the universe, a sense of appreciation is the foundation of all acts of piety and, ultimately, saintliness. Indigenous cultures of many continents also draw heavily upon this concept, using it as a launching pad for their daily acts and their very existence.

Native American tribes lived their existence on this country's plains, woodlands and prairies for centuries before the age of exploration. Central to their beliefs is gratitude and respect for everything around them–the seen and unseen. Key rituals focus on the vital importance of giving back to the tribal family, Mother Earth and the Great Spirit. Nothing is taken from the earth without being replaced. Thanks is given for every blessing, suffering and seemingly insignificant act. Tribal customs that cross all indigenous traditions center on giving something back, no matter how small or trivial. This reinforces an innate sense of thankfulness among the individual as well as within the tribe.

Paralleling that, Zen Buddhists define a happy life by several characteristics—humility, labor, service, prayer and gratitude. The key, of course, is gratitude. According to Zen writings, the mark of a useless person is lack of appreciation. *"The unworthy man is ungrateful, forgetful of benefits [done to him]. This ingratitude, this forgetfulness is congenial to mean people… But the worthy person is grateful and mindful of bene-*

fits done to him. *This gratitude, this mindfulness, is congenial to the best people."*

The indigenous peoples of Africa also share in this tradition. Prayers are said upon the slaying of prey, offering thanks to the animal for giving its life so that the tribe can live. The tribe then honors that prayer by wasting none of the carcass.

∽

"One upon whom we bestow kindness, but will not express gratitude, is worse than a robber who carries away our belongings."

— Yoruba (Nigeria) Proverb

The Vietnamese Buddhist priest, Thich Nhat Hanh, impresses upon his listeners to embrace life by becoming fully aware. Awareness, he says, is the essence of living. When we are aware, we appreciate our life. We become aware of our power to love and be peaceful. He cautions: don't pray for what we already have or can do ourselves. For instance, don't pray for peace. Instead, be peace. Become the living testament and the embodiment of peace.

Those in the Muslim faith pray five times a day. Their morning supplication includes a time of meditation, preparation and appreciation. They reflect on their deeds, but always defer to Allah with gratitude and appreciation for all that confronts them. They confess that there is nothing they have done that was not made possible except through the Divine, Eternal Presence of Allah. And for that, they are eternally grateful.

Not only has gratitude been the basis for most religions, the power of gratitude as a healing agent has been historically known. The Japanese tradition of Naikan, which literally translates into "seeing oneself with the mind's eye," was developed by a Buddhist monk, and uses deep introspection to look at a person's life in the minutest detail, highlighting all those individual instances from the smallest deeds to the largest. Appreciation for the most minute is a crucial first step, as collectively, all those tiny deeds are instrumental to our very existence.

∽

Gratitude is so all-encompassing, it can transform our lives into ones of great meaning and ultimately, joy. The quest for a life of happiness lies in the answer to the question—how do we nurture that sacred place of thankfulness in our soul?

Chapter II

Living a Life
of Gratitude

"*A grateful mind is*
eventually attracts t

great mind that

t great things."

– Plato

life lived in the state of gratitude is marked by sterling human qualities, namely, generosity of spirit, deep and abiding hope, a broad life perspective, trust in the divine balance of the universe, intrinsic humility, and an absence of petty hatreds and jealousies.

Albert Schweitzer, Mahatma Ghandi, Mother Teresa were all individuals who lived and breathed a life philosophy of gratitude. All of them, according to Robert Emmons, professor of psychology at the University of California-Davis and an authority on the topic of gratitude, have much in common.

"They don't seem to fit the usual conception of gratitude where you see a benefit and then you're grateful. They felt grateful for the opportunity to help, as opposed to receiving help. They knew there was some benefit for them in developing compassion or whatever it was, and so they didn't need to receive gratefulness from the people they helped. I think what enabled them to persist under stressful circumstances was just the ability to be helpful, which created in them a sense of gratitude, a sense of purpose, that they wouldn't otherwise have had."

There is no coincidence that these individuals are spiritually-driven beings. All of them have a deeper faith in something greater than themselves. And all of them not only preached valuable life lessons based on the gratitude, but lived them as well.

ALBERT SCHWEITZER

(JANUARY 14, 1875–SEPTEMBER 4, 1965)

"Success is not the key to happiness. Happiness is the key to success. If you love what you are doing, you will be successful."

Humanitarian, theologian, missionary, concert organist, and medical doctor, Albert Schweitzer is predominately known for his selfless life that was centered around his belief that all things, living and breathing, deserved deep respect. Schweitzer was born in Alsace, which at the time was part of Germany. Remarkably, by the age of 21, Schweitzer had decided the course of his life. For nine years he would dedicate himself to the study of science, music, and theology. Then he would devote the rest of his life to serving humanity directly. And indeed, before he was 30, he was a respected writer on theology, an accomplished organist, and an authority on the life and work of Johann Sebastian Bach.

In 1904 Schweitzer was inspired to become a medical missionary after reading an evangelical paper regarding the needs of medical missions. He studied medicine from 1905 to 1913 at the University of Strasbourg. He also raised money to establish a hospital in French Equatorial Africa. As a trained medical doctor, he went to Africa in 1913 with his wife to establish a hospital near an already existing mission post. In his lifetime, Schweitzer remained true to the promise he had made to himself as a young man, treating thousands of patients and devoting special care to the lepers of Africa.

Schweitzer's world view was based on the idea of respect for life He wrote about this simple but profound concept in *"Reverence for Life,"* which he believed to be his greatest single contribution to humankind. His view was that Western civilization was in decay because it was gradually abandoning its ethical foundation - the affirmation of life. It was his firm conviction that the respect for life is the highest principle. He persistently emphasized the necessity of thoughtful living, rather than merely acting on the basis of passing impulses or by following the most widespread opinions. Respect for life, resulting from contemplation of one's own conscious will to live, leads the individual to live in the service of other people and of every living creature.

Schweitzer was very much respected for putting his theory into practice. He won the Nobel Peace Prize in 1952, and used the money from the honor to start a hospital and sanctuary for lepers. Schweitzer died in Africa in 1965 after years of serving others.

MAHATMA GANDHI

(OCTOBER 2, 1869-JANUARY 30, 1948)

"Civilization, in the real sense of the term, consists not in the multiplication but in the deliberate reduction of wants. This alone promotes real happiness and contentment."

If anyone has been able to master the concept of simplifying life, it was Gandhi. Born Mohandas Karamchand Gandhi in India, he was a national icon who led the struggle for India's independence from British colonial rule, empowering tens of millions of common Indians. Throughout his life he opposed any form of terrorism or violence, instead using only the highest moral standards. His philosophy of nonviolence has since influenced and inspired resistance movements all over the world. Civil rights activist Martin Luther King modeled his peaceful protests after Gandhi's example and succeeded in firing a movement that resonates in America to this day. Gandhi created a serenity about himself because of his deep gratitude for what he had. And what did he have? Quite frankly, nothing. He gave up his practice of law as a young man, which, given his keen mind and depth of understanding of the human condition, could have made him a very powerful and wealthy man. But he found power and internal wealth another way. Living an austere life, he denied himself nearly of all personal possessions. He ate very little, fasted often and abstained from physical relations with his wife for most of his marriage. He was known to use nonviolent forms of protest to challenge world violence, including extreme hunger strikes that left him on the verge of death.

From the time he took charge of the freedom struggle and the Indian National Congress in 1918, he was lovingly revered as "Mahatma," or "Great Soul" by millions of Indians, although he was disliked honorary titles. By his nonviolent civil disobedience, Gandhi helped bring about India's independence from British rule, inspiring other colonial peoples to work for their own independence and ultimately dismantling the British Empire. Gandhi's principle of satyagraha (from Sanskrit; *satya* for truth and *agraha* for endeavor), often translated as "way of truth" or "pursuit of truth." Gandhi often stated that his principles were simple; drawn from traditional Hindu beliefs. As Gandhi said: "I have nothing new to teach the world. Truth and nonviolence are as old as the hills."

MOTHER TERESA

(AUGUST 26, 1910-SEPT. 5, 1997)

"The miracle is not that we do this work, but that we are happy to do it."

Therein lies the secret benefit of gratitude. By being appreciative of life in all its many varying aspects, Mother Teresa was able to create a synergy in the people she worked with, imbuing their toil with joy. To the many she touched, she was a saint. Selflessness was her internal motivator; she had the ability to see one person's suffering as a microcosm of global need.

Mother Teresa was born Agnes Gonxha Bojaxhiu in 1910 in Yugoslavia. She joined the Sisters of Loreto in 1928, and took the name "Teresa" after St. Teresa of Lisieux, patroness of the missionaries.

In 1948, she came across a half-dead woman lying in front of a Calcutta hospital. She stayed with the woman until she died. From that point on, she dedicated the majority of her life to helping the poorest of the poor in India, thus gaining her the name "Saint of the Gutters." She founded an order of nuns called the Missionaries of Charity in Calcutta, India, dedicated to serving the poor. Almost 50 years later, the Missionaries of Charity have grown from 12 sisters in India to over 3,000 in 517 missions throughout 100 countries worldwide.

In 1952, she founded the Nirmal Hriday Home for the Dying in a former temple in Calcutta. It was there that they would care for the dying Indians that were found on the streets. It didn't matter whether they were dying of AIDS or leprosy. Her goal was to enable them to die in peace and with dignity. That devotion towards the poor won her respect throughout the world and the Nobel Peace Prize in 1979.

JOHN MUIR

(APRIL 21, 1838–DEC. 24, 1914)

"When we try to pick out anything by itself, we find it hitched to everything else in the Universe."

Undeniably, John Muir was America's most famous and influential naturalist and conservationist. He has been called "The Father of our National Parks," "Wilderness Prophet," and "Citizen of the Universe." But he once described himself more humorously, and perhaps most accurately, as, a "poetico-trampo-geologist-botanist and ornithologist-naturalist, etc. etc."

Muir understood the interconnectedness of life–that no one thing happens in the universe without it affecting the whole. Perhaps this was why he was so passionate as a naturalist. His drive to protect the land and preserve the natural beauty of California was a reflection of his greater appreciation for nature.

Born in Scotland, Muir moved to the states in 1849 at the age of eleven, where they eventually settled in Wisconsin. In 1867, while working at a carriage parts shop in Indianapolis, Muir suffered a blinding eye injury that would change his life. When he regained his sight one month later, Muir resolved to turn his eyes to the fields and woods–and thus began his love affair with nature. He spent years as a wanderlust. He walked a thousand miles from Indianapolis to the Gulf of Mexico. He sailed to Cuba, and later to Panama, where he crossed the Isthmus and sailed up the West Coast, landing in San Francisco in March, 1868. From that moment on, though he would travel around the world, California became his home.

As a wilderness explorer, he is renowned for his exciting adventures in California's Sierra Nevada, among Alaska's glaciers, and world-wide travels in search of nature's beauty. As a prolific writer, his writings contributed to the creation of Yosemite, Sequoia, Mount Rainier, Petrified Forest, and Grand Canyon National Parks.

His worked inspired President Theodore Roosevelt's innovative conservation programs, including establishing the first National Monuments by Presidential Proclamation, and Yosemite National Park by congressional action. In 1892, John Muir and other supporters formed the Sierra Club "to make the mountains glad." John Muir was thec Club's first president, an office he held until his death in 1914. His last battle to save the second Yosemite, Hecht Hetchy Valley failed. But that lost battle ultimately resulted in a widespread conviction that our national parks should be held inviolate. In the face of rampant industrialism, Muir stood apart. His bowed to nature, and kept that theme of gratitude central to his life's mission. "The clearest way into the Universe is through a forest wilderness."

DALAI LAMA

(JULY 6, 1935–)

"I am just a simple Buddhist monk, no more, nor less."

As a spiritual leader, the Dalai Lama has followed the path of Buddhism. As the 14th Dalai Lama, he is believed to be manifestations of Avalokiteshvara or Chenrezig, the Bodhisattva of Compassion and patron saint of Tibet. As a bodhisattva, he is considered an enlightened being who has postponed his own nirvana and chosen to take rebirth in order to serve humanity. In this capacity, his is life of service and gratitude, seeking a higher path in which to lead humanity.

A fascinating story, the Dalai Lama was born Lhamo Thondup to a poor family in the small village of Taktser in the province of Amdo, Tibet. He lived in a small, poor settlement that stood on a hill overlooking a broad valley. One of sixteen children, of whom only seven lived, he was taken from his family when he was barely three. A search party sent out by the Tibetan government to find the new incarnation of the Dalai Lama arrived at the monastery in his town following a series of interpretations of signs that they believed would lead them to the correct person. It was deemed that he was indeed the 14th incarnation and was officially installed in 1940. Like his predecessors, the Dalai Lama was the head of the Tibetan government, controlling a large portion of the country until he was exiled in 1959 when the People's Republic of China maintained rule over Tibet. He currently resides in northern India. This gave him the position of the Tibetan independence movement.

Politics aside, the Dalai Lama has grown to be a respected and revered figure in modern history because of his life philosophy, which is centered around the austere lifestyle of a Tibetan Buddhist monk. It is built on gratitude and servitude. His belief that all forms of life are to be preserved. Even in the face of his detractors and opponents, he shows respect and bows to the enlightened, god nature within them. It is this basic belief–continually taking the higher road but never giving in to authority– that has gained him wide popularity and appeal. He walks the path with goodness and kindness.

In 1989 he was awarded the Nobel Peace Prize for his non-violent struggle for the liberation of Tibet. Like Ghandi, consistently advocated policies of non-violence, even in the face of extreme aggression. "This is my simple religion. There is no need for temples; no need for complicated philosophy.

Our own brain, our own heart is our temple; the philosophy is kindness."

All those who walk in the light of gratitude are living examples of the philosophies they preached. Their beliefs were more than just a series of memorable quotes, or moving speeches. They were living, breathing, applicable ways of life that helped them attain something that we all are strive for and that is internal happiness and peace. They cultivated to an art the state of being known as gratitude, being thankful for the least that life had to offer, which drew to them great abundance.

Chapter III

The LifeLesson
Principles of Gratitude

"No one is as capabl

who has emerged from

of gratitude as one

the kingdom of night.

— Elie Wiesel

1) FIND YOUR ABUNDANCE, AND HONOR IT.

"If you judge people, you have no time to love them."

— Mother Teresa

Whether you look at the glass half empty or half full, the fact remains that the glass still contains something. And that something is abundance. Perception is everything. If you don't think there is anything in your life that is worthy of gratitude, if you only focus on what you don't have, then it's time to think again. Central to developing a spirit of gratitude is re-framing your perception. You can start by living in the moment.

- **Be specific.** Did someone deliver your paper to your house this morning? Did a clerk hand you back your change at the counter? Was your coffee hot and fresh at the diner? You could argue that they were just "doing their jobs," but the point is, job or not, those simple acts benefited you today. Perhaps you have come to take the small things for granted. Being thankful for small things is the seedling of gratitude. If you were to look at every single aspect of your day, and trace exactly how many people made those details go smoothly—regardless of intent–you would have thousands of people to thank by nightfall. It is so easy to ignore the things that go right every minute of every day, even if it's just that the earth continues to spin on its axis and the sun is still coming up. But allowing the missteps of life to capture all of our attention allows all of our energy to become negative. Reverse the negativity by concentrating first on the small gifts, and finally on the grander gifts, that are within our reach at all times..

- **We are all in this together.** Take a look at your own role in everyday life, too. If someone cuts you off while driving, it immediately makes you angry. But if you do the same thing to someone else, your first thought might be, I didn't mean it. Well, how do you know the other fellow didn't mean it, either? Don't let there be a disconnect between what you see and experience and what the intent or lack of it might be.

Approach others with understanding. We've all done things we are not proud of. Let's learn from them by accepting their role in our lives, and allow them to give us greater understanding of each other. If you didn't attach judgment to the things that happen to you in the course of a day...if you just let life unfold, and appreciated it in its unfolding, where might you be right now? The truth is, no one is out to get you. Let go of what you think life should be, and be open to what it is. Actively seek out the abundance in your life each day. Give something back -- a smile, a nod, a simple thank you. Make someone's life richer by giving them a gift even before they do anything to deserve it.

2) THERE IS A DIVINE BALANCE IN THE UNIVERSE.

"One of the great things about the universe is that it's fair."
— Alan Bean

f you're one of those people who believes that life is a hardship, then the last thing you want to hear is that life is fair and there is a balance in the universe. People have a tendency to let a very painful experience define the rest of their existence. A nasty divorce, a wretched childhood, the loss of a child or spouse, an addiction or other horrible life experience can become the door through which everything else passes, and by which everything else in life becomes tainted. It is unfair to you and it is unfair to the experience. When enough of these life experiences pile up, it can jade our view of the universe as being a just and fair place. Well, the truth is that it is. There are some basic concepts to help you understand that.

- **You don't have all the information.** Our view, no matter how well-traveled or savvy we are, is myopic. Most of us only know life through our individual experiences. We interpret situations and sequences of events based on our own limited bank of knowledge. But it is really just the tip of the iceberg, because in most situations, we have very little knowledge of the rest of the story. Nor, often, do we care. We sometimes cling stubbornly to the belief that something was done to us, deliberately or unfairly. Medical intuit Carolyn Myss tells a story about a soldier held in a prison camp for years during World War II. His German guard would enter his cell daily and force a mixture of maggots and other bugs down his throat. It wasn't until later in life that he discovered what was really happening. The guard was not trying to torture him; rather, he was trying to keep him alive, by feeding him something, anything he could find. The moral to the story: There is always much more information that you may never know. Trust that what is happening to you has purpose. Perhaps one day, if you're lucky, you will indeed be able to put it all into context. The scales will always balance. Trust that.

- **Entitlement will kill you.** If our premise as humans is that we are deserving of something better, then there is an entitlement issue here that may or may not be warranted. Who says you are deserving? At the risk of posing another rhetorical question, if everyone feels the way you do—that life has shortchanged them—then can't it be argued that the universe is entirely fair? We all feel like we deserve something more. Face it, all of us have the same hand dealt to us, with some variations. The truth is most likely that all of us—bar none—experience hardships, turmoil, anguishing losses, abject disappointments and a variety of other unpleasant, unhappy things. Our role is to accept what happens to us and to do what we can with the possibilities that life offers us. Acceptance is the key to this. If we can stop trying to figure out what we did wrong to warrant the problems that we face, and just accept it as part of what happens while living on this planet, we can find immense freedom. Life is what it is. And if we can reach unconditional acceptance of that, then the door to true gratitude will open.

3) YOU ARE UNIQUE, BUT YOU ARE CERTAINLY NOT ALONE.

"A hundred times a day I remind myself that my inner and outer life depends on the labors of other men, living and dead, and that I must exert myself in order to give in the measure as I have received and am still receiving."

Albert Einstein

his could be better called understanding the concept of universal welfare. This requires embracing the idea of a larger interconnectedness between us as fellow humans, creating a unity with the planet and atmosphere which we ultimately all share. It embraces the 'we' rather than the 'me.'

- **What happens to each of us is a microcosm of the greater whole.** In the Torah, it states that if you save one person, you save humanity. Our actions, although seemingly individual and isolated, are actually impacting the course of humanity. It's a heavy thought, but many religions and spiritualists believe in the ripple effect of actions.

Since none of us can exist in a vacuum, the concept is integral not only to the survival of our species and our universe but to its renaissance as well. Many humanitarians and philanthropists have an underlying belief that, in doing good on a local or regional level, they are helping to create a larger synergy that ultimately will benefit all of humanity. No act of kindness, therefore, is without greater meaning. When you choose the higher path and present the "better you" in even the smallest situation, it does set the wheels in motion to create a better, more beautiful world. Even if it just seems like it's only your world that is being changed, trust that it's much bigger than you know.

- **Nothing goes unnoticed.** Christians believe that man's law is nothing compared to God's law. Everything is written on the universal tablet. So even if no one sees you breaking a law or doing something that shows the lesser side of you, the greater knowledge, God, sees it. Drawing upon spiritualism and Buddhism, the same concept is known loosely as karma—the sum total of all thoughts, words and deeds. Even those from previous lives are tallied, according to Buddhist belief. Cause and effect is central to that belief. Every action has a reaction. Even if you don't see it or feel it, it is there. The idea that the universe keeps an ongoing accounting of what we do or don't do supports the concept that life is expansive. All our acts, from the most insignificant to the most grandiose, are registered. But the miraculous aspect to this idea is that for those who act out of generosity and selfless-ness, feeling truly thankful for all that life presents, the effects are immediate. We begin to feel not only the happiness that those intrinsic characteristics can bring, we feel the joy in the moment of doing them. And we begin to feel that interconnectedness with others that allows us to reach out, embrace, relate and feel a part of the greater humanity around us in the form of one single person.

4) Unearthing gratitude in sorrow and in pain.

"I want to know if you have touched the center of your own sorrow, if you have been opened by life's betrayals or have become shriveled and closed from fear of further pain."

Oriah Mountain Dreamer

hile the universe is balanced and fair, that's not to say it always seems that way. Especially in the wake of a tragedy, personal or global, life's harshest aspects seem unredeemed. To get to a place where sorrow and pain can't touch us is not realistic. The enormity of loss is so complicated and oppressive that it is not something that can be put into perspective without Herculean effort and intense internal battles. To get to a level of acceptance comes from back-breaking soul searching. You never get over loss. But to understand the purpose it has within our life, well, that is indeed possible. The first step to developing gratitude, even in the face of unbearable sorrow, is acceptance.

- **Tragedy has many victims.** If someone we love is ill, it not only affects the person who is ill but also those who love him. First, as those who love that person, we have to accept the tragedy, with all of its frightening and painful implications. This is a grueling process, because it requires us to reach into our fear, our sadness and our pain and walk through it. We have to feel the pain, not avoid it. If we do not understand what is happening within ourselves and what that will mean to us in the future, there is no way we can fundamentally integrate this experience into our lives. It also keeps us from being able to help and comfort our loved one and others. We cannot extend any true help without doing this. Second, we need to allow others to walk their own path. Accept and be thankful for the fact that others will have their own unique reactions. They have their own processes and their own ways of coping and dealing. Acceptance of what is allows you to let them do what they need to do in their own time. You cannot change another person, or their responses. You can only allow them time and space to deal with personal loss and sorrow on their own terms. Walk with them, not in front of them. Be gracious and grateful for that opportunity.

- **Every painful event that happens to you serves you.** It's natural to be angry, furious, disheartened, distraught, even to feel destroyed over painful situations that happen to us. The hardest part is to be thankful to those people or events that we perceive have hurt us. There is a generosity in forgiveness that is possibly the hardest to experience. But since generosity is often the first step to gratitude, and vice versa, it is not impossible–in fact, it is highly probable–to go beyond those feelings and get to the other side. It takes time. The first step is to understand that you truly are not alone. It is virtually not possible to go through life unscathed, without experiencing that which is very painful. Allowing these painful experiences to hollow you out, rather than helping you to plumb the depths of your own character, can make you a miserable person. Look outside yourself and find comfort that your experience is shared by thousands, if not millions of others. Accept that you truly had no control over it. Give yourself time and dig deep. Find the answers that are there. Go forth in courage.

5) GRATITUDE IS POWER.

"If you don't give a bit of yourself to someone else, you are a failure."

Robert Mastruzzi

ratitude is such a powerful tool, namely because it erases fear. Fear of what? Fear of the unknown. When we can truly embrace our entire life–the good, the bad, and even the ugly, although it can be argued that there is no ugly if you have a healthy perspective–then the unknown doesn't stand a chance. For some reason, even

though, if asked, any of us could regale a crowd with all the bad things that have happened to us in the course of our lives, very few of us actually learn by them. We often complain about them, let them block us from moving forward and enjoying life, and use them only for the perverse pleasure of rehashing them over and over. But if we did what was precisely intended of them, and that is let those experiences pile up and create a ballast for our ship, we could sail more smoothly through the choppy waters.

- ## Gratitude is a large emotion. When you feel true appreciation for someone, it minimizes all the negatives in your life. It takes up a lot of space in your soul, if you are doing it right. It swells and fills the emptiness and pushes out the bad. Buddhist scripture (teachings?) says 'Even a room that has been dark for a thousand years can be lighted by one single candle.' Starting with a small bit of gratitude for a small benefit is the place to start. Compiling that with continued acts of gratitude, saying thank you to everyone, and meaning it, looking past small offenses, reframing setbacks and ending your day reflecting on all that is good in your world–all of that builds and strengthens gratitude. If you can truly get to that place where you walk in a state of gratitude, you have nothing to fear because you have gained perspective on your life.

- Gratitude is contagious. By its very nature, thankfulness is warm and embracing. You don't have to go around hugging everyone, but when you give a thank you to someone, mean it. Say it with intent and warmth, and watch the smile and energy of that person change.

Give it as a gift. It has a power of its own that can change a person's day, even the course of their life. There are many accounts of people who, on the brink of committing suicide, have heard that one word of thanks, and it was just enough to keep them going. Being appreciated is a vital, life-sustaining need that once met has a tremendous domino effect.

6) GRATITUDE BEGETS GRATITUDE – THE LAW OF ATTRACTION.

"Watch your thoughts; they become words. Watch your words; they become actions. Watch your actions; they become habits. Watch your habits; they become character. Watch your character; it becomes your destiny."

— Frank Outlaw

Thought, word and deed. Thought is just as powerful as deed, so you should be vigilant even about how you think. This is the kernel of belief behind the law of attraction. Simply put, it says: Like attracts like. The theory is that thoughts are energy and act like magnets, drawing to them thoughts of similar vibration. When enough thoughts accumulate upon a given topic, it is drawn into the life experience. Emotions also play into this, acting as amplifiers to thought, adding what theorists describe as vibration, or vibrational energy patterns. Powerful emotions, both positive or negative, will draw thoughts more quickly into the life experience. While positive thoughts generate positive emotions and draw positive life experiences, negative do the reverse.

- **Gratitude, like love, has a very high frequency.** So basically speaking, the more appreciative you are, the more will come to you. As Ralph Marston writes, "What if you gave someone a gift, and they neglected to thank you for it—would you be likely to give them another? Life is the same way. In order to attract more of the blessings that life has to offer, you must truly appreciate what you already have." The more appreciation you can generate internally in the way of feelings, as well as externally in the manner of deed, the more appreciation you create in and for your own life. The synergistic effect of upgrading your level of gratitude creates a vortex so that much positive comes to you. Those around you will treat you as you have treated them. The more gratitude and generosity you shower on the world, the more it will shower on you.

"*Gratitude unlocks the fullness of life. It turns what we have into enough, and more. It turns denial into acceptance, chaos to order, confusion to clarity. It can turn a meal into a feast, a house into a home, a stranger into a friend. Gratitude makes sense of our past, brings peace for today, and creates a vision for tomorrow.*" — Melody Beattie

Chapter IV

Quotes & Wisdom for Living a Life of Gratitude

> "*Blessed is he who*
>
> *for he shall not be*

expects no gratitude,

disappointed."

— *W. C. Bennett*

"With mindfulness, every moment of every day is a precious jewel."

— Thich Nhat Hanh

QUOTES AND WISDOM FOR LIVING A LIFE OF GRATITUDE

"Our love of what is beautiful does not lead to extravagance; our love of things of the mind does not make us soft."

— Pericles

"Gratitude makes us more human "ubuntu." We can re-claim our know the Source of our life. guilt and shame because we make us perfect, little gods. We are made mistakes, but we can turn our mistakes into For that, we can be thankful."

QUOTES AND WISDOM FOR LIVING A LIFE OF GRATITUDE

what the Zulus in South Africa call humanity, our ubuntu, because we We don't need to burden ourselves with mistakes. The Creator did not make human. We err. We make earning moments and opportunities.

— Rev. Arthur Cribbs

" As I walk, as I walk The universe is walking with me In beauty it walks before me In beauty it walks behind me In beauty it walks below me In beauty it walks above me Beauty is on every side As I walk, I walk with Beauty. "

— Ancient Navajo Prayer

QUOTES AND WISDOM FOR LIVING A LIFE OF GRATITUDE

"What is called sympathy, kindness, mercy, goodness, pity, compassion, gentleness, humanity, appreciation, gratefulness, and service—in reality, it is love."

— Pir-O-Murshid Hazrat Inayat Khan

"To see a *world* in a Grain of Sand, And a Heaven in a Wild Flower, Hold **Infinity** in the palm of your hand, And *eternity* in an *hour*."

— William Blake

"Dickinson called "a blossom of the brain"
and William Blake described as "seeing the
world in a grain of sand, eternity in an
hour," of crucial moments in which, as
James Joyce put it, "the soul of the com-
monest object…seems to us as radiant."

— Richard Heinberg

"Blessed are those that can give without

remembering and receive without forgetting."

— Author Unknown

QUOTES AND WISDOM FOR LIVING A LIFE OF GRATITUDE

"Thank God — every morning when you get up—that you have something to do which must be done, whether you like it or not. Being forced to work, and forced to do your best, will breed in you a hundred virtues which the idle never know."

— Charles Kingsley

"A contented mind is the greatest blessing a man can enjoy in this world."

— Joseph Addison

"If you concentrate on finding whatever is good in every situation, you will discover that your life will suddenly be filled with gratitude, a feeling that nurtures the soul."

— Rabbi Harold Kushner

"He is a wise man who does not grieve for the things which he has not, but rejoices for those which he has."

— Epictetus

"The sun was shining in my eyes, and I

could barely see

To do the necessary task that was allotted me.

Resentment of the vivid glow, I started to

complain —

When all at once upon the air I heard the

blindman's cane."

— Earl Musselman

"You simply will not be the same person two months from now after consciously giving thanks each day for the abundance that exists in your life. And you will have set in motion an ancient spiritual law: the more you have and are grateful for, the more will be given you..."

— Sarah Ban Breathnach

QUOTES AND WISDOM FOR LIVING A LIFE OF GRATITUDE

"Gratitude is not only the greatest of virtues, but the **parent** of all the others."

—Cicero

"As we express our

never forget that the

is not to utter words,

gratitude, we must highest appreciation ut to live by them."

— John Fitzgerald Kennedy

"To speak gratitude is courteous and pleasant, to enact gratitude is generous and noble, but to live gratitude is to touch Heaven.

— Johannes A. Gaertner

QUOTES AND WISDOM FOR LIVING A LIFE OF GRATITUDE

"To *educate yourself* for the feeling of gratitude means to take **nothing for granted,** but to always seek out and value the kind that will stand behind the action. Nothing that is done for you is a matter of course. Everything originates in a **will for the good,** which is directed at you. Train yourself never to put off the word or action for the *expression of gratitude."* — Albert Schweitzer

"Most of us, swimming against the tides of

need only a bit of praise or encouragement —

rouble the world knows nothing about,

nd we will make the goal."

— Jerome P. Fleishman

"Every time we **remember** to say "*thank you,*" we experience nothing less than **heaven** on earth."

— Sarah Ban Breathnach

"**Nothing** is more **honorable** than a *grateful heart.*

— Seneca

QUOTES AND WISDOM FOR LIVING A LIFE OF GRATITUDE

"Gratitude is something of which none of us can give too much. For on the smiles, the thanks we give, our little gestures of appreciation, our neighbors build their philosophy of life."

— A. J. Cronin

"*There is a calmness*

gratitude, *a*

QUOTES AND WISDOM FOR LIVING A LIFE OF GRATITUDE

to a *life* lived in

quiet joy."

— Ralph Blum

"People are like stained-glass windows. They sparkle and shine when the sun is out, but when the darkness sets in their true beauty is revealed only if there is a light from within."

— Elizabeth Kubler-Ross

"All that we are is the result of what we have thought. The mind is everything. What we think, we become."

— Maharishi Mahesh Yogi

"Don't put the key to your happiness in someone else's pocket."

— Swami Chinmayanandaji

Chapter V

About
The LifeLessons
Foundation™

Thank you for supporting The LifeLessons Foundation™, a charitable foundation devoted to helping those struggling along on their journey in life. By purchasing this book, you have supported the Foundation, as part of the proceeds is earmarked to fund this worthy cause.

The LifeLessons Foundation™ is based on five principles:

- Live gratitude. We started The LifeLessons Foundation™ in gratitude for the many blessings in our lives. People seldom stop to count their blessings, and it is even more rare when we stop to help others in need. The LifeLessons Foundation™ believes that as individuals and as communities we must help others less fortunate. It is our obligation and our joy.

- Take action. It is a central belief at LifeLessons that kindness and caring are not simply words, but a course of action in how we must live our lives as individuals and as communities. For our Foundation, no cause may be too small so long as it supports the growth of the individual or family.

- **Give back.** We also believe that each of us has been blessed with special qualities in our character that can benefit others. Each of us has a purpose in life; often we are at our best when we are helping others. There are many charitable organizations doing great work around the world. We strive to be one of them.

- **Focus on a universe of one.** The LifeLessons Foundation™ is devoted to helping those in need, those who may be overlooked, forgotten or unaware that the world does care about their personal struggles. Whether it is a parent balancing the needs of a terminally ill child and a full-time job, or a family living in poverty but struggling to rise above the squalor – The LifeLessons Foundation™ is trying to help – one person, one family, one community at a time.

• **Celebrate life.** In joy and in sorrow, we at LifeLessons™ try to celebrate life in all its forms. And giving is indeed the best way to herald that celebration. Make a difference by donating to The LifeLessons Foundation™. Visit us on the web at www.lifelessons.org or write to us at:

The LifeLessons Foundation™
12 Port Farm Road
Kennebunkport, ME 04046

About the Author

Lifelong fan of gratitude, **Lenore Skomal** is also the author of *The Secret Life of Girlfriends* (Cider Mill Press), *Heroes: Fifty Stories of the American Spirit*, and *Keeper of Lime Rock*, which won national recognition. An award-winning humor columnist, journalist and professor of writing, she resides in Pennsylvania with her son and husband.

About Cider Mill Press Book Publishers

Good ideas ripen with time. From seed to harvest, Cider Mill Press strives to bring fine reading, information, and entertainment together between the covers of its creatively crafted books. Our Cider Mill bears fruit twice a year, publishing a new crop of titles each Spring and Fall.

Visit us on the web at
www.cidermillpress.com
or write to us at
12 Port Farm Road
Kennebunkport, Maine 04046

CIDER MILL
PRESS

BOOK
PUBLISHERS

*Where Good Books
are Ready for Press*